Christian Gratitude Journal

Grateful, Thankful, Blessed
5 minutes a day, for 90 days

Christian Gratitude Journal

Grateful, Thankful, Blessed
5 minutes a day, for 90 days

Abigail Miller

KALOGRIA PRESS

ISBN: 9798497284744

Note

Would you like to know about upcoming books and promotions from Kalogria Press?

Whenever we publish a new book, we like to give away a dozen copies as a way of saying thank you to our readers

If you enjoy this journal and would like the chance to receive one of our future giveaway copies, then please email us your name and postal address to kalogriapress@gmail.com and we will enter you into the next draw.

NB. We will never share your personal details with anyone… ever.

Continue your journey with God at
www.kalogriapress.com

How to use this journal

Gratitude is one of the cornerstones of our faith – there are countless verses in the Bible that urge us to thank and praise God for all his greatness, for the blessings he brings to our lives.

Declaring our thanks for God's presence in our lives keeps us in check spiritually. With gratitude we can acknowledge the things we already have; over the things we want.

When we truly know how blessed we are, we let go of our own ego and appreciate that there is so much good in our lives that happens *for* us, not because of us.

When we bring true gratitude into our hearts, we can ease any bitterness in our hearts: we can see that many of the challenges in our lives – whilst they cannot be avoided – can be overcome. And therein lies the greatest gift to be thankful for: God's strength that allows us to persevere.

And it's not just our faith that calls for us to be grateful. Behavioral scientists all agree that people who regularly experience and consciously express gratitude enjoy great mental health benefits: practicing gratitude improves the lives of those with depression, anxiety, and low self-esteem.

Of course, when our lives are busy, complicated, or faced with immense challenges, it can be difficult to keep hold of that gratitude: daily trials leave us exhausted or weigh us down and we forget to look outside of our problems or take time to be grateful for the things that *are* good in our lives.

This is why I've written this journal. It has been designed to help you find a simple way to reconnect with gratitude, for just 5 minutes every day over 90 days.

This journal is arranged in weekly sections; each week has:

• An inspirational image to start the week
- if you have a few extra minutes, you can color and meditate on the image and its message, if you wish.

• 7 daily pages, each page has
- a Scripture verse to focus your gratitude.
- three gratitude prompts where can you jot down one or two responses.

• A reflection page to end the week
- use this page to look back on the past week's gratitude prompts and note what you've learned so far, and what you're looking forward to in the week to come

My hope is that when you get to the end of your three-month gratitude journal, the lessons you have learnt will be firmly placed in your heart.

For where your treasure is, there your heart will be also. ~ Matthew 6:21

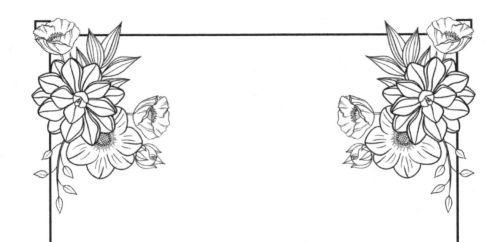

This journal belongs to

date_____/_____/_____

For everything God created is good, and nothing is
to be rejected if it is received with thanksgiving.
~ 1 Timothy 4:4

Something that went well today

_____

_____

_____

A friend who makes me laugh

_____

_____

_____

Something in my life that I'm fortunate to have

_____

_____

_____

date_____/_____/_____

I will give thanks to you, Lord, with all my heart; I will
tell of all your wonderful deeds.
~ Psalm 9:1

Someone in my life that supports and loves me

_____

_____

_____

A freedom that I'm grateful for

_____

_____

_____

Something beautiful I saw today

_____

_____

_____

date_____/_____/_____

So then, just as you received Christ Jesus as Lord,
continue to live your lives in Him, rooted and built up in Him,
strengthened in the faith as you were taught, and overflowing
with thankfulness. ~ Colossians 2:6-7

Something difficult that made me a better person

_____

_____

_____

An opportunity in my life that I've been blessed to receive

_____

_____

_____

A reason to smile right now

_____

_____

_____

date_____/_____/_____

Do not be anxious about anything, but in every situation, by prayer and petition, with thanksgiving, present your requests to God. ~ Philippians 4:6

Something positive that happened today

_____

_____

_____

Something I worried about that turned out fine

_____

_____

_____

Home comforts that I am grateful for

_____

_____

_____

date_____/_____/_____

… serve him faithfully with all your heart; consider
what great things he has done for you.
~ 1 Samuel 12:24

Something funny that happened recently

_____

_____

_____

Something good that happened without me doing anything

_____

_____

_____

Strangers who have shown me kindness

_____

_____

_____

date_____/_____/_____

The Lord is my shepherd, I lack nothing. He makes
me lie down in green pastures, he leads me beside
quiet waters, he refreshes my soul. ~ Psalm 23:1-6

Someone who loves me

_____

_____

_____

Something I take for granted every day that makes my life wonderful

_____

_____

_____

Something that I have today that no one had 50 years ago

_____

_____

_____

date_____/_____/_____

And we know that in all things God works for the good of those who love him, who have been called according to his purpose. ~ Romans 8:28

Something nice that I was able to do for someone

_____

_____

_____

Something new I learned

_____

_____

_____

The best thing about my life right now

_____

_____

_____

Grateful, Thankful, Blessed

What have I learnt this week?

_____
_____
_____
_____
_____
_____
_____
_____
_____
_____
_____
_____
_____

What do I still have to learn?

_____
_____
_____
_____
_____
_____

date_____/_____/_____

But I trust in your unfailing love;
my heart rejoices in your salvation.
~ Psalm 13:5

Something I'm grateful for at the very start of the day

_____

_____

_____

Someone or something that made today a good day

_____

_____

_____

A favorite memory that I cherish

_____

_____

_____

date_____/_____/_____

Through Jesus, therefore, let us continually offer to God a sacrifice of praise—the fruit of lips that openly profess his name. ~ Hebrews 13:15

Food or drink that I'm grateful to receive today

_____

_____

_____

People who do jobs that I appreciate

_____

_____

_____

Something I get to have that not everybody gets to have

_____

_____

_____

date_____/_____/_____

And whatever you do, whether in word or deed, do it all in the name of the Lord Jesus, giving thanks to God the Father through him. ~ Colossians 3:17

Something on my to do list that got done

_____

_____

_____

Someone, some place, or something that made me happy today

_____

_____

_____

What can I be happy about right now?

_____

_____

_____

date_____/_____/_____

I have not stopped giving thanks for you,
remembering you in my prayers.
~ Ephesians 1:16

Friends who've stood by me

_____

_____

_____

Something that I accomplished today

_____

_____

_____

A moment that helped me feel peace

_____

_____

_____

date_____/_____/_____

For God so loved the world that he gave his one and only Son, that whoever believes in him shall not perish but have eternal life. ~ John 3:16

A valuable lesson I've learned

_____
_____
_____

Something I did that made me feel proud of myself

_____
_____
_____

Choices that I get to make

_____
_____
_____

date_____/_____/_____

In the same way, let your light shine before others,
that they may see your good deeds and glorify your
Father in heaven. ~ Matthew 5:16

My best quality, for which I'm grateful

_____

_____

_____

Someone who inspires me

_____

_____

_____

Something or someone that made me laugh today

_____

_____

_____

date_____/_____/_____

Blessed is she who has believed that the Lord
would fulfill his promises to her!
~ Luke 1:45

Something difficult I've overcome

_____

_____

_____

A mistake that helped me grow

_____

_____

_____

Something fun I got to do today

_____

_____

_____

Grateful, Thankful, Blessed

What have I learnt this week?

_____

_____

_____

_____

_____

_____

_____

_____

_____

_____

_____

_____

_____

_____

What do I still have to learn?

_____

_____

_____

_____

_____

_____

Courage

date_____/_____/_____

I have learned the secret of being content in any and every situation, whether well fed or hungry, whether living in plenty or in want. I can do all this through him who gives me strength. ~ Philippians 4:12-13

Something I'm grateful for today

_____

_____

_____

Something positive that happened today

_____

_____

_____

Something in my life that I'm fortunate to have

_____

_____

_____

date_____/_____/_____

It is good to praise the Lord and make music to your name, O Most High, proclaiming your love in the morning and your faithfulness at night. ~ Psalm 92:1-2

Something I'm grateful for at the very start of the day

_____

_____

_____

Something beautiful I saw today

_____

_____

_____

A blessing I received today

_____

_____

_____

date_____/_____/_____

Give thanks to the Lord, for he is good; his love
endures forever. ~ 1 Chronicles 16:34

Friends who lift me up

_____

_____

_____

An opportunity in my life that I've been blessed to receive

_____

_____

_____

A good memory that I can hold onto

_____

_____

_____

date_____/_____/_____

… I take part in the meal with thankfulness… whether you eat or drink or whatever you do, do it all for the glory of God. ~ 1 Corinthians 10:30-31

Food or drink that I enjoyed today

_____

_____

_____

Someone in my life that supports and loves me

_____

_____

_____

Something difficult I have overcome

_____

_____

_____

date_____/_____/_____

Everywhere and in every way…
we acknowledge this with profound gratitude.
~ Acts 24:3

A mistake that helped me grow

_____

_____

_____

Someone who inspires me

_____

_____

_____

A freedom that I'm grateful for

_____

_____

_____

date_____/_____/_____

Enter his gates with thanksgiving and his courts with praise;
give thanks to him and praise his name. For the Lord is good
and his love endures forever; his faithfulness continues
through all generations. ~ Psalm 100:4-5

Something that went well today

_____

_____

_____

Something good that happened without me doing anything

_____

_____

_____

The best thing about my life right now

_____

_____

_____

date_____/_____/_____

… always giving thanks to God the Father for
everything, in the name of our Lord Jesus Christ.
~ Ephesians 5:20

Something I worried about that turned out fine

_____

_____

_____

Someone, some place, or something that made me happy today

_____

_____

_____

Home comforts that I'm grateful for

_____

_____

_____

Grateful, Thankful, Blessed

What have I learnt this week?

_____
_____
_____
_____
_____
_____
_____
_____
_____
_____
_____
_____
_____

What do I still have to learn?

_____
_____
_____
_____
_____

Patience

date_____/_____/_____

Consider it pure joy, my brothers and sisters, whenever you face trials of many kinds, because you know that the testing of your faith produces perseverance.
~ James 1:2-3

Something difficult that made me a better person

_____

_____

_____

Something that I accomplished today

_____

_____

_____

A reason to smile right now

_____

_____

_____

date_____/_____/_____

I will give you thanks in the great assembly; among
the throngs I will praise you.
~ Psalm 35:18

A friend who makes you laugh

_____

_____

_____

People who do jobs that I appreciate

_____

_____

_____

Choices that I get to make

_____

_____

_____

date_____/_____/_____

For where your treasure is,
there your heart will be also.
~ Matthew 6:21

One thing I appreciate about myself

_____

_____

_____

People who have shown me kindness

_____

_____

_____

A good thing that happened today

_____

_____

_____

date_____/_____/_____

Let us come before him with thanksgiving and
extol him with music and song.
~ Psalm 95:2

A song that cheers my spirit

_____

_____

_____

Something nice that I was able to do for someone

_____

_____

_____

Something I take for granted every day that makes my life easier

_____

_____

_____

date_____/_____/_____

There are different kinds of gifts,
but the same Spirit distributes them.
~ 1 Corinthians 12:4

Something I do well

_____
_____
_____

Something or someone that made me laugh today

_____
_____
_____

A moment that strengthened my faith

_____
_____
_____

date_____/_____/_____

Devote yourselves to prayer,
being watchful and thankful.
~ Colossians 4:2

Someone or something that made today a good day

_____

_____

_____

Something on my to do list that got done

_____

_____

_____

Something new I learned

_____

_____

_____

date_____/_____/_____

Save us, Lord our God, and gather us from the
nations, that we may give thanks to your holy name
and glory in your praise. ~ Psalm 106:47

Something I did that made me feel proud of myself

_____

_____

_____

Something fun I got to do today

_____

_____

_____

What can I be happy about right now?

_____

_____

_____

Grateful, Thankful, Blessed

What have I learnt this week?

_____

_____

_____

_____

_____

_____

_____

_____

_____

_____

_____

_____

_____

What do I still have to learn?

_____

_____

_____

_____

_____

date_____/_____/_____

Not only so, but we also glory in our sufferings, because
we know that suffering produces perseverance;
perseverance, character; and character, hope.
~ Romans 5:3-4

Something difficult I have overcome

_____

_____

_____

Something nice that I was able to do for someone

_____

_____

_____

Something positive that happened today

_____

_____

_____

date_____/_____/_____

May he give you the desire of your heart
and make all your plans succeed.
~ Psalm 20:4

Something on my to do list that got done

_____

_____

_____

Something inspirational I watched or read recently

_____

_____

_____

A good decision I made

_____

_____

_____

date_____/_____/_____

Let the message of Christ dwell among you richly as you
teach ... with all wisdom through psalms, hymns, and songs
from the Spirit, singing to God with gratitude in your hearts.
~ Colossians 3:16

Something or someone that made me smile today

_____

_____

_____

A person in my life that I've been blessed to know

_____

_____

_____

A moment that helped me feel hopeful

_____

_____

_____

date_____/_____/_____

For what you have done I will always praise you in the presence of your faithful people. And I will hope in your name, for your name is good. ~ Psalm 52:9

Something I take for granted every day that makes me happy

_____

_____

_____

Something that went well today

_____

_____

_____

A valuable lesson I've learned

_____

_____

_____

date_____/_____/_____

Rejoice always, pray continually, give thanks in all
circumstances; for this is God's will for you in
Christ Jesus. ~ 1 Thessalonians 5:16-18

What can I be happy about right now?

_____

_____

_____

Something good that happened without me doing anything

_____

_____

_____

A freedom that I'm grateful for

_____

_____

_____

date_____/_____/_____

Let them give thanks to the Lord for his unfailing love
and his wonderful deeds for mankind, for he satisfies the
thirsty and fills the hungry with good things.
~ Psalm 107:8-9

Food that nourished me today

_____

_____

_____

Someone I can rely on

_____

_____

_____

Someone or something that made today a good day

_____

_____

_____

date_____/_____/_____

Every good and perfect gift is from above, coming down from the Father of the heavenly lights, who does not change like shifting shadows. ~ James 1:17

Someone who loves me

_____

_____

_____

A positive story from my past

_____

_____

_____

Daily comforts that I'm grateful for

_____

_____

_____

Grateful, Thankful, Blessed

What have I learnt this week?

_____
_____
_____
_____
_____
_____
_____
_____
_____
_____
_____
_____
_____

What do I still have to learn?

_____
_____
_____
_____
_____
_____

date_____/_____/_____

Let them give thanks to the Lord for his unfailing love and his wonderful deeds for mankind. Let them sacrifice thank offerings and tell of his works with songs of joy.
~ Psalm 107:21-22

Someone I love

_____

_____

_____

Something beautiful I saw today

_____

_____

_____

Something in my life that I'm fortunate to have

_____

_____

_____

date_____/_____/_____

Therefore we do not lose heart. Though outwardly we are wasting away, yet inwardly we are being renewed day by day. ~ 2 Corinthians 4:16

Something I can be grateful for every morning

_____

_____

_____

Something I worried about that turned out fine

_____

_____

_____

Someone in my life that supports and loves me

_____

_____

_____

date_____/_____/_____

But blessed are your eyes because they see,
and your ears because they hear.
~ Matthew 13:16

The best thing about my life right now

_____

_____

_____

A friend who I'm always happy to see

_____

_____

_____

Essential services that I appreciate

_____

_____

_____

date_____/_____/_____

Give thanks to the Lord, for he is good;
his love endures forever.
~ Psalm 106:1

A person who went the extra mile for me

_____

_____

_____

A mistake that helped me grow

_____

_____

_____

Something in my life that I'm fortunate to have

_____

_____

_____

date_____/_____/_____

Because of the Lord's great love we are not consumed,
for his compassions never fail. They are new every
morning; great is your faithfulness.
~ Lamentations 3:22-23

Something I did that made me feel proud of myself

_____

_____

_____

Something that calms me

_____

_____

_____

Something I did today that I would like to do again

_____

_____

_____

date_____/_____/_____

I will extol the Lord at all times;
his praise will always be on my lips.
~ Psalm 34:1

A book I could read again and again

_____

_____

_____

A reason to smile right now

_____

_____

_____

Something fun I got to do today

_____

_____

_____

date_____/_____/_____

Come to me, all you who are weary and burdened,
and I will give you rest.
~ Matthew 11:28

Something that I accomplished today

_____

_____

_____

A time when I have felt complete peace

_____

_____

_____

A burden I have been able to let go

_____

_____

_____

Grateful, Thankful, Blessed

What have I learnt this week?

_____
_____
_____
_____
_____
_____
_____
_____
_____
_____
_____
_____
_____
_____

What do I still have to learn?

_____
_____
_____
_____
_____

Joy

date_____/_____/_____

… and giving joyful thanks to the Father, who has qualified you to share in the inheritance of his holy people in the kingdom of light. ~ Colossians 1:12

Someone, some place or something that made me happy today

_____

_____

_____

A liberty that I enjoy

_____

_____

_____

The best thing about my life right now

_____

_____

_____

date_____/_____/_____

The Lord has done it this very day;
let us rejoice today and be glad.
~ Psalm 118:24

People who have been kind to me

_____

_____

_____

An opportunity in my life that I've been blessed to receive

_____

_____

_____

Someone or something that brings me joy

_____

_____

_____

date_____/_____/_____

But I, with shouts of grateful praise, will sacrifice to you. What I have vowed I will make good. I will say, "Salvation comes from the Lord." ~ Jonah 2:9

Sacrifices I have made that were worth it

_____

_____

_____

A valuable lesson I've learned

_____

_____

_____

Something that went well today

_____

_____

_____

date_____/_____/_____

Rejoice in the Lord, you who are righteous,
and praise his holy name!
~ Psalm 97:12

Someone in my life that supports and loves me

_____

_____

_____

Something joyful that happened recently

_____

_____

_____

Something I take for granted every day that makes my life wonderful

_____

_____

_____

date_____/_____/_____

Therefore, since we are receiving a kingdom that cannot
be shaken, let us be thankful, and so worship God
acceptably with reverence and awe. ~ Hebrews 12:28

The best thing about my life right now

_____

_____

_____

Something that I accomplished today

_____

_____

_____

Something in nature that fills me with awe

_____

_____

_____

date_____/_____/_____

Taste and see that the Lord is good; blessed is the
one who takes refuge in him.
~ Psalm 34:8

Delicious food or drink that I get to enjoy

_____

_____

_____

Something or someone that made me laugh today

_____

_____

_____

Home comforts that I'm grateful for

_____

_____

_____

date_____/_____/_____

You will be enriched in every way so that you can be generous on every occasion, and through us your generosity will result in thanksgiving to God.
~ 2 Corinthians 9:11

Something helpful that I was able to do for someone

_____

_____

_____

Someone who has been generous towards me

_____

_____

_____

Something in my life that I'm fortunate to have

_____

_____

_____

Grateful, Thankful, Blessed

What have I learnt this week?

_____
_____
_____
_____
_____
_____
_____
_____
_____
_____
_____
_____
_____
_____

What do I still have to learn?

_____
_____
_____
_____
_____

date_____/_____/_____

The Lord is my strength and my shield; my heart trusts in him, and he helps me. My heart leaps for joy, and with my song I praise him. ~ Psalm 28:7

A time that I felt strong

_____

_____

_____

Something positive that happened today

_____

_____

_____

Choices that I get to make

_____

_____

_____

date_____/_____/_____

I will praise God's name in song
and glorify him with thanksgiving.
~ Psalm 69:30

Music that fills me with joy

_____

_____

_____

My best quality, for which I'm grateful

_____

_____

_____

Something fun I got to do today

_____

_____

_____

date_____/_____/_____

Light in a messenger's eyes brings joy to the heart,
and good news gives health to the bones.
~ Proverbs 15:30

What I've done to look after my health today

_____

_____

_____

Something difficult I have overcome

_____

_____

_____

A friend who makes you laugh

_____

_____

_____

date_____/_____/_____

I will give thanks to the Lord because of his righteousness; I will sing the praises of the name of the Lord Most High. ~ Psalm 7:17

Someone or something that made today a good day

_____

_____

_____

Something I did that made me feel proud of myself

_____

_____

_____

Something new I learned

_____

_____

_____

date_____/_____/_____

But thanks be to God! He gives us the victory
through our Lord Jesus Christ.
~ 1 Corinthians 15:57

Something good that happened without me doing anything

_____

_____

_____

People who support me

_____

_____

_____

Something I get to have that not everybody gets to have

_____

_____

_____

date_____/_____/_____

I thank and praise you, God of my ancestors: You have
given me wisdom and power, you have made known
to me what we asked of you, you have made known
to us the dream of the king. ~ Daniel 2:23

Something difficult that made me a better person

_____

_____

_____

People who serve my daily needs, who I appreciate

_____

_____

_____

Something on my to do list that got done

_____

_____

_____

date_____/_____/_____

I will sacrifice a freewill offering to you;
I will praise your name, Lord, for it is good.
~ Psalm 54:6

Something I'm grateful for at the very start of the day

_____

_____

_____

Someone, some place or something that made me happy today

_____

_____

_____

Something I feared that turned out fine

_____

_____

_____

Grateful, Thankful, Blessed

What have I learnt this week?

_____
_____
_____
_____
_____
_____
_____
_____
_____
_____
_____
_____

What do I still have to learn?

_____
_____
_____
_____
_____

date_____/_____/_____

For it is by grace you have been saved, through
faith—and this is not from yourselves,
it is the gift of God. ~ Ephesians 2:8

Something that went well today

_____

_____

_____

Someone in my life that supports and loves me

_____

_____

_____

Something difficult that made me a better person

_____

_____

_____

date_____/_____/_____

Praise the Lord, my soul; all my inmost being,
praise his holy name.
~ Psalms 103:1

The best thing about my life right now

_____

_____

_____

Something beautiful I saw today

_____

_____

_____

Someone who inspires me

_____

_____

_____

date_____/_____/_____

I always thank my God for you because of his
grace given you in Christ Jesus.
~ 1 Corinthians 1:4

What can I be happy about right now?

_____

_____

_____

Something useful I got to do today

_____

_____

_____

Something good that happened without me doing anything

_____

_____

_____

date_____/_____/_____

Thanks be to God for his indescribable gift!
~ 2 Corinthians 9:15

Something positive that happened today

_____

_____

_____

A gift I've been able to give someone

_____

_____

_____

A way that I can be more help to others

_____

_____

_____

date_____/_____/_____

I will praise you, Lord my God, with all my heart;
I will glorify your name forever.
~ Psalm 86:12

Something I'm grateful for at the very start of the day

_____

_____

_____

A valuable lesson I've learned

_____

_____

_____

Something I take for granted every day that makes my life wonderful

_____

_____

_____

date_____/_____/_____

For although they knew God, they neither glorified him as
God nor gave thanks to him, but their thinking became futile
and their foolish hearts were darkened. ~ Romans 1:21

An opportunity in my life that I've been blessed to receive

_____
_____
_____

A freedom that I'm grateful for

_____
_____
_____

A reason to smile right now

_____
_____
_____

date_____/_____/_____

All this is for your benefit, so that the grace that is reaching
more and more people may cause thanksgiving to overflow
to the glory of God. ~ 2 Corinthians 4:15

Someone or something that made today a good day

_____

_____

_____

Something that I accomplished today

_____

_____

_____

A moment that helped me feel God's grace

_____

_____

_____

Grateful, Thankful, Blessed

What have I learnt this week?

_____
_____
_____
_____
_____
_____
_____
_____
_____
_____
_____
_____
_____
_____

What do I still have to learn?

_____
_____
_____
_____
_____
_____

date_____/_____/_____

With praise and thanksgiving they sang to the Lord: "He is good; his love toward Israel endures forever." And all the people gave a great shout of praise to the Lord, because the foundation of the house of the Lord was laid. ~ Ezra 3:11

A mistake that helped me grow

_____

_____

_____

Someone who loves me

_____

_____

_____

Something difficult I have overcome

_____

_____

_____

date _____ / _____ / _____

How many are your works, Lord! In wisdom you
made them all... will sing to the Lord all my life; I will sing
praise to my God as long as I live. ~ Psalm 104:24-33

Something I get to have that not everybody gets to have

_____

_____

_____

Something inspirational I watched or read recently

_____

_____

_____

Modern conveniences that I'm grateful for

_____

_____

_____

date_____/_____/_____

Sing to the Lord, for he has done glorious things; let
this be known to all the world. ~ Isaiah 12:5

Something funny that happened recently

_____

_____

_____

Something I worried about that turned out fine

_____

_____

_____

Something I did that made me feel proud of myself

_____

_____

_____

date_____/_____/_____

Praise the Lord, my soul, and forget not all his benefits ...
who redeems your life from the pit and crowns you with
love and compassion. ~ Psalm 103:2-5

Something or someone that made me laugh today

_____

_____

_____

Something new I learned

_____

_____

_____

Friends I love

_____

_____

_____

date_____/_____/_____

...Let the light of your face shine on us.
Fill my heart with joy...
~ Psalm 4:6-7

Something or someone in my life that I'm fortunate to have

_____

_____

_____

Strangers who have shown me kindness

_____

_____

_____

Decisions that I get to make

_____

_____

_____

date_____/_____/_____

May the Lord repay you for what you have done. May you be richly rewarded by the Lord, the God of Israel, under whose wings you have come to take refuge. ~ Ruth 2:12

A time when I felt appreciated

_____

_____

_____

Something I managed to do today

_____

_____

_____

Something that I have today that no one had 50 years ago

_____

_____

_____

date_____/_____/_____

I rejoice in following your statutes as one rejoices in great riches… I delight in your decrees; I will not neglect your word. ~ Psalm 119:14-16

People who do jobs that keep me safe

_____

_____

_____

A person who is always there for me

_____

_____

_____

A memory that I am thankful to have

_____

_____

_____

Grateful, Thankful, Blessed

What have I learnt this week?

_____

_____

_____

_____

_____

_____

_____

_____

_____

_____

_____

_____

_____

_____

_____

What do I still have to learn?

_____

_____

_____

_____

_____

_____

date_____/_____/_____

In that day you will say: Give praise to the Lord, proclaim
his name; make known among the nations what he has
done, and proclaim that his name is exalted.
~ Isaiah 12:4

Something I'm grateful for at the very start of the day

_____

_____

_____

Someone, some place, or something that made me happy today

_____

_____

_____

Something that went well today

_____

_____

_____

date_____/_____/_____

Then we your people, the sheep of your pasture, will praise you forever; from generation to generation we will proclaim your praise. ~ Psalm 79:13

Something that I have today that no one had 50 years ago

_____

_____

_____

An opportunity in my life that I've been blessed to receive

_____

_____

_____

What can I be happy about right now?

_____

_____

_____

date_____/_____/_____

Save us, O God of our salvation, and gather and deliver us … that we may give thanks to your holy name, and glory in your praise. ~ 1 Chronicles 16:35

Something or someone that made me laugh today

_____

_____

_____

Someone in my life that supports and loves me

_____

_____

_____

A valuable lesson I've learned

_____

_____

_____

date_____/_____/_____

Sing to the Lord with grateful praise;
make music to our God on the harp.
~ Psalm 147:7

Something fun I got to do today

_____
_____
_____

Something that I accomplished today

_____
_____
_____

The best thing about my life right now

_____
_____
_____

date_____/_____/_____

Hallelujah! For our Lord God Almighty reigns. Let us rejoice and be glad and give him glory!
~ Revelation 19:6-7

Something good that happened without me doing anything

_____

_____

_____

People who do jobs that I appreciate

_____

_____

_____

Something positive that happened today

_____

_____

_____

date_____/_____/_____

Give praise to the Lord, proclaim his name.
~ 1 Chronicles 16:8

Something I take for granted every day that makes my life easier

_____

_____

_____

A moment that helped me feel at ease

_____

_____

_____

Someone or something that made today a good day

_____

_____

_____

date_____/_____/_____

For you created my inmost being; you knit me together in my mother's womb. I praise you because I am fearfully and wonderfully made; your works are wonderful, I know that full well. ~ Psalm 139:13-14

My best feature, for which I'm grateful

_____

_____

_____

Something difficult I have overcome

_____

_____

_____

A reason to smile right now

_____

_____

_____

Grateful, Thankful, Blessed

What have I learnt this week?

_____
_____
_____
_____
_____
_____
_____
_____
_____
_____
_____
_____
_____

What do I still have to learn?

_____
_____
_____
_____
_____
_____
_____

date_____/_____/_____

May the Lord now show you kindness and
faithfulness, and I too will show you the same favor
because you have done this. ~ 2 Samuel 2:6

Something positive that happened recently

_____
_____
_____

Something good that I was able to do for someone

_____
_____
_____

Something or someone that I have faith in

_____
_____
_____

date_____/_____/_____

God is within her, she will not fall;
God will help her at break of day.
~ Psalm 46 :5

Someone I can trust

_____

_____

_____

A freedom that I'm grateful for

_____

_____

_____

Something I worried about that turned out fine

_____

_____

_____

date_____/_____/_____

But blessed is the one who trusts in the Lord, whose confidence is in him. They will be like a tree planted by the water that sends out its roots by the stream.
~ Jeremiah 17:7-8

Strangers who have shown me kindness

_____

_____

_____

Something in my life that I'm blessed to have

_____

_____

_____

Something difficult that made me a better person

_____

_____

_____

*date*_____/_____/_____

Rejoice in the Lord and be glad, you righteous;
sing, all you who are upright in heart!
~ Psalm 32:11

A friend who makes you laugh

_____

_____

_____

Something new I learned

_____

_____

_____

Something I get to have that not everybody gets to have

_____

_____

_____

date_____/_____/_____

We ought always to thank God for you, brothers and sisters,
and rightly so, because your faith is growing more and more,
and the love all of you have for one another is increasing.
~ 2 Thessalonians 1:3

Something I did that made me feel proud of myself

_____

_____

_____

Choices that I get to make

_____

_____

_____

Someone who inspires me

_____

_____

_____

date_____/_____/_____

Blessed are those who keep his statutes
and seek him with all their heart.
~ Psalm 119:2

Home comforts that protect me

_____

_____

_____

Something I worried about that turned out fine

_____

_____

_____

A good thing that happened today

_____

_____

_____

date_____/_____/_____

The shepherds returned, glorifying and praising
God for all the things they had heard and seen,
which were just as they had been told. ~ Luke 2:20

Something good I didn't believe, but ended up being true

_____

_____

_____

Someone who makes an effort for me

_____

_____

_____

Something beautiful I saw today

_____

_____

_____

Grateful, Thankful, Blessed

What have I learnt this week?

_____
_____
_____
_____
_____
_____
_____
_____
_____
_____
_____
_____
_____
_____

What do I still have to learn?

_____
_____
_____
_____
_____
_____

Peace

date_____/_____/_____

Let the peace of Christ rule in your hearts, since as
members of one body you were called to peace.
And be thankful. ~ Colossians 3:15

Something that brings me peace every day

_____

_____

_____

The best thing about my life right now

_____

_____

_____

Something difficult I have overcome

_____

_____

_____

date_____/_____/_____

You are worthy, our Lord and God, to receive glory and
honor and power, for you created all things, and by your
will they were created and have their being.
~ Revelation 4:11

Something positive that happened today

_____

_____

_____

Something in my life that I'm fortunate to have

_____

_____

_____

A moment that helped me feel peace

_____

_____

_____

date_____/_____/_____

Many waters cannot quench love;
rivers cannot sweep it away.
~ Songs of Solomon 8:7

Something I'm grateful for at the very start of the day

_____

_____

_____

Something beautiful I saw today

_____

_____

_____

Someone who loves me

_____

_____

_____

date_____/_____/_____

Glory to God in the highest heaven, and on earth
peace to those on whom his favor rests.
~ Luke 2:14

Someone or something that made today a good day

_____

_____

_____

An opportunity in my life that I've been blessed to receive

_____

_____

_____

A freedom that I'm grateful for

_____

_____

_____

date_____/_____/_____

But godliness with contentment is great gain. For we brought
nothing into the world, and we can take nothing out of it. But
if we have food and clothing, we will be content with that.
~ 1 Timothy 6:6-8

Something that I have today that no one had 50 years ago

_____

_____

_____

Food or drink that I'm grateful to receive today

_____

_____

_____

What can I be happy about right now?

_____

_____

_____

date_____/_____/_____

Therefore do not worry about tomorrow, for
tomorrow will worry about itself. Each day has
enough trouble of its own. ~ Matthew 6:34

Something I worried about that turned out fine

_____

_____

_____

Something good that happened without me doing anything

_____

_____

_____

A mistake that helped me grow

_____

_____

_____

date_____/_____/_____

The Lord bless you and keep you; the Lord make his face shine on you and be gracious to you; the Lord turn his face toward you and give you peace.
~ Numbers 6:24-26

Something I get to have that not everybody gets to have

_____

_____

_____

A favorite memory that I cherish

_____

_____

_____

A reason to smile right now

_____

_____

_____

Grateful, Thankful, Blessed

What have I learnt this week?

_____
_____
_____
_____
_____
_____
_____
_____
_____
_____
_____
_____
_____
_____

What do I still have to learn?

_____
_____
_____
_____
_____
_____
_____

Thank you!

This journal is published by Kalogria Press, an independent publishing house run by husband-and-wife team, Grace and Jamie Sandford.

Kalogria Press focuses on providing Christian devotionals, guided journals and prayer books that speak to our experiences on our journey through faith. We hope that this journal has brought you closer to God.

If there is anything we could do to make this book more useful to you, please get in touch at kalogriapress@gmail.com and help us to improve future editions.

Continue your journey with God at www.kalogriapress.com

Finally, if you have enjoyed this book, please support us by leaving a review. Here is a direct link to the review page on Amazon: www.kalogriapress.com/thanks

Thank you and God bless

Also from Kalogria Press

www.kalogriapress.com/seeking-serenity

In these complicated times, where many aspects of our lives - our health, our families, our communities, our jobs - seem to be in jeopardy, it's easy to feel overwhelmed by uncertainty and fear.

By exploring how the Scriptures have enabled her to find peace when confronted with tragedy and uncertainty in her own life, Grace Sandford offers you this devotional and guided journal.

Week by week, this journal will help you face your fears, bring them to God and find the serenity in faith to live an anxiety free life!

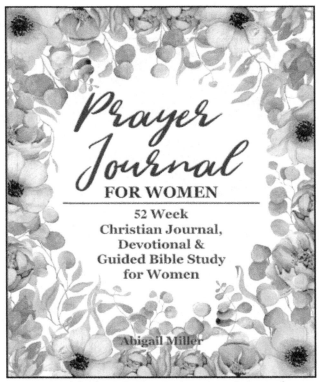

www.kalogriapress/prayer-journal

A compact 52-week Devotional & Guided Bible Study for Women includes:

Scripture verses, Reflections, guided spaces to write about your Gratitude, ask for Guidance, note your Prayers and Blessings, and Illustrations on every page for you to color if you wish.

This beautiful journal is also organized into six key themes to guide your journey:
- Hope & Resilience
- Faith & Trust
- Love & Gratitude
- Perseverance
- Doubt & Fear
- Courage & Wisdom

Perfect for both individual devotion and group Bible study.
Start your journey with God today!

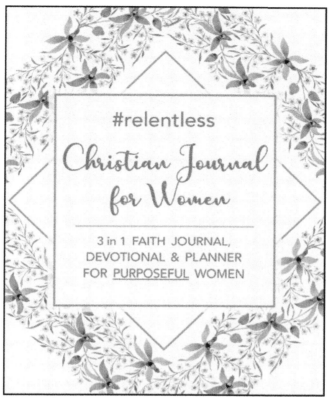

www.kalogriapress.com/relentless-journal

Does it feel like a Christian woman's work is never done!? If your life feels #relentless then this is the Christian woman's devotional journal for you.

• 3-in-1 prayer journal, daily devotional, and weekly planner

• Covers 52 weeks
• Reflect with devotional scripture verse
• Journal your prayers and give thanks
• Note your important appointments and things to do

Keep everything on track
and remain relentlessly committed to Christ!